CHANGING YOUR PARADIGM TO THE CHRIST MIND

Strategies for Empowerment Part 1

Keith E. Jackson, MA, MFT

authorHOUSE®

AuthorHouse™
1663 Liberty Drive
Bloomington, IN 47403
www.authorhouse.com
Phone: 1-800-839-8640

Published by AuthorHouse   03/28/2013

ISBN: 978-1-4634-0034-7 (sc)
ISBN: 978-1-4634-0033-0 (e)

Library of Congress Control Number: 2011908050

Erin Krewson, Today's Hype Designs.com and cover photo by Keith Jackson

I dedicate this book, to all those people, who have sacrificed their lives for the cause of the Gospel of Christ. If it were not for their selfless acts, I would not have known the wonderful gift God has given me. I pray that I will do the same for my generation.

TABLE OF CONTENTS

PREFACE

This book started out as an outline for a leadership conference that I was to facilitate. However, as I began to prepare the subject matter, I was flooded with spiritual insights from the Holy Spirit. Before I knew it, an outline turned into a book. I had wanted to write a book, but I had something totally different in mind. In fact, I still intend on writing that book, but I have learned that it is not my will but the will of God that I need to follow.

I wrote a majority of this book during an extended fast. Maybe that is why my spiritual insights were so clear and the creative forces so strong. The title of this book says it all. The message that I am attempting to convey to the reader, is to exam your cognitive (thought) processes to see how valid they are. Are there thoughts that you have accepted because of the status quo? Have those thoughts become strongholds that prevent you from growing in your spiritual walk?

Are you satisfied with your spiritual life? Do you feel that you are living the life that God has called you to live? Have you read promises from the bible, and thought they were for only a selected few, and not you? Do you believe in the promises of God; that He has given to those who call upon His name? Are you experiencing those promises in your life?

If you are like me, the answer to the majority of the aforementioned questions was no. Yes, from the world's perspective, I was successful. I had the career, the house, and the lifestyle most people would envy, but I knew God had called me for so much more. I read the promises of God, and I realized that most of my prosperity was a false prosperity. I was one paycheck from financial disaster. Sure, I made more money than 80% of the population, but most of it went to creditors.

I was living like the Hebrews in the wilderness, surviving day by day in this world's system. We all have to go through our wilderness experiences, but it is not God's design that we stay there. Eventually, He wants to lead you into the promise land. God wants you to experience heaven on this earth. (Due 11:21)

Once I came to this realization, I began to seek the guidance of the Holy Spirit, to show me; what I needed to change my paradigm to the Christ mind. It is only when we think, the way Jesus thought, can we do what Jesus did. (John 14:12) I know this is a radical statement for some of you, but I am taking Jesus at His word. I believe the Word of God is true, and God is not a man that He should lie. (Heb 6:18)

As a Psycho-Therapist, I know the connection between thoughts, beliefs, and actions. What we believe, we will perceive, and what we perceive, we will act upon. With this knowledge, I began to put together this book, for those people like myself; that want to fulfill the vision God has for them in this life. This means, to be in a position to help the fatherless; weak and needy, and assist the destitute and the afflicted. (Psalms 82:3-4)

As is my style, this book is not too lengthy. I chose to disclose principles rather than get into specifics. I find if a person learns the principles, they can apply them, to whatever situation they might face. I have also included scriptures along with the text for reference. I encourage you to read the scripture references, for yourself, and allow the Spirit of God to speak to you.

I am confident that the information in this book, if applied, will work for you as it has done for me. Be strong in the Lord and the Power of His Might.

ACKNOWLEDGMENTS

This is my opportunity to thank some people for making this possible. First of all, I thank God, for without Him this book would not have been written. Next, I would like to thank my parents, for without them, I would not be here. They also loved me and instilled the principles of success, which I needed in order to strive in this world. I also would like to thank Carlene, for all her support through the years. Finally, Love and Thanks to my children, Jared and Cassandra; you have inspired me beyond words; Jane, you have always been in my corner. Thanks also to San Diego County Probation and Sheriff Department, to Dr. Barry Lord and all my professors and teachers at Southern California Bible College, Al Houghton, who's teachings and life have been an example of how a real Man of God should live and think, to Pastor Derrick Traylor and Rehoboth World Healing Center for your prayers and intercession; to Kenneth Copeland, Fred K. Price, Creflo Dollar, Bill Winston, Marilyn Hickey, Leroy Thompson, Mike Murdock, and Zachery Tims who's teachings have touched me and made me what I am today. Oh yes, thanks to Jimmy Long for leading me to the LORD. Last but not least, I cannot leave out my friends and some of my enemies; because you have provided comfort or made me strong.

CHANGING OUR PARADIGM TO THE CHRIST MIND

This book is designed to challenge your mind set and kick down some of the sacred cows that hinder you from becoming all that God has created you to be. In the Gospel of John, Jesus made a profound statement. Jesus stated that all the works he had done, his disciplines could do; and even greater works, because he was returning to His heavenly father. (John 14:12-14) Was Jesus serious when he said this? Some may say that he was speaking figuratively, but I am of the opinion that this statement was a literal one. There are numerous scriptures to back up my contention. If Jesus was serious, are you experiencing the power and authority that Jesus said was available to all those who call on his name? If the answer is no, then, why aren't you?

It is my contention, in order for us to be trusted with that kind of power and authority we must develop the same mind set that Jesus had. In the book of Romans, the apostle Paul, under the inspiration of the Holy Spirit, encouraged the believers to renew their minds. (Romans 12:1-3) Paul realized that in order to experience the power and authority that God has for us we need to learn to think a different way. We need to learn a new paradigm. Many believers are living life far below what God has intended for them. Some have rationalized that this is their plight, and they endure the hardships, with the hope someday that they will get their reward in the sweet by and by. This sounds real religious and many would applaud this mind set. But is it truly scriptural?

The enemy would love nothing more than for believers to think this way. Why? Because, they are no threat to him. He can continue to beat them upside the head with little or no resistance at all. No, God's design for you is to be a king and priest on this earth (Rev 1:5-6). God has created you to have dominion on this earth (Gen 1:26). In the gospel of Mark, Jesus commissioned his followers to go out and make disciples, cast out demons, and heal the sick. (Mark 16:14-18) On another occasion Peter complained to Jesus that he had given all to follow him. Jesus responded by telling him all who have given up their worldly possessions and lifestyle to follow him would get back a hundred times that amount; not only in heaven, but in this life. (Mark 10:17-31)

If you are not experiencing the aforementioned, don't you think it's time to ask why? If you are satisfied with your life, this book is not for you. In fact, I admire you. I wish I could be that content, but I am not! I want to experience all that God has for me. I want to be blessed so I can be a blessing according to the promise God gave Abraham. You know that all those who are of the faith of Abraham are entitled to the same blessings of Abraham? Maybe, that is the problem; you didn't know.

In the following pages, we are going to look at ways we can renew our minds, and challenge our current cognitive processes. The subjects that we will cover are the following:

What does it mean to be responsible?

What is the difference between responsibility and accountability

What is God's purpose for you?

Are you a prisoner of your past or a pioneer of your future?

Living life from an internal locus of control.

Thinking outside of the box.

Using your hardships to your advantage.

Turning your dreams into reality (the process for change).

Strategies for success.

ARE YOUR TRADITIONS GETTING IN YOUR WAY?

One of the reasons why you might not be experiencing the fullness God has for you, is your traditions. What are traditions? Can you think of some traditions that you have? One tradition I can think of is eating turkey for Thanksgiving. Think of how many turkeys are consumed during this holiday (55 million), Why? Is it because of the tradition that has been passed down from generation to generation? What traditions have you accepted that have been passed down? Some traditions are neutral in nature. However, there are some traditions that can be a stumbling block to us.

The problem with traditions is that they can become a truth unto themselves. What do I mean by that? Some people are so indoctrinated by their traditions that they do not even question if this tradition is valid, or why does that tradition exist. We, as humans, are creatures of habit. We like to have a routine, so it is easy for us to fall prey to tradition. As I previously stated, not all traditions are bad, but there are those traditions that can hinder you. For example, Jesus and his disciples were seen by some religious people eating kernels of grain while they walked through a field. It was the religious tradition not to work on the Sabbath day. The religious people were quick to criticize them, for this was a perceived transgression against God's laws. However, Jesus was quick to point out to them that they were the ones who were guilty of not following the Word of God. He concluded that you make the Word of God of no effect because of your traditions. (Mat 15:1-20)

What does this abovementioned encounter demonstrate? It shows how powerful traditions are. They can blind us to the truth and become such a stronghold in our minds that we cannot see the truth, even when it is staring us in the face. Why were the religious people of Jesus' day so offended by him? Some were afraid of him because they found him to be a threat to their traditions and their power (John 11:47-48). Others were offended because he did not fit the mold of what they perceived the Messiah to be. (Matt 13:53-58) In either case, they were unable to benefit from the encounter with Jesus.

How many in our churches today, fall into the same category as the Pharisees? How many people, because of their traditions or mindset, are not allowing the power and the anointing to flow in their lives? Is this true of yourself? Are you allowing your traditions to rob you of the blessings God has for you? In the follow pages, I will share some information with you that you might find challenging to your mindset. I only ask that you open your mind and not allow the birds to eat the seeds that are being spread on the soil of your mind. (Mark 4:4)

STRONGHOLDS OF THE MIND

Sometimes it's not the enemy that gets in the way of our success, it is ourselves. Our own thought processes can prevent the blessings God has for us from manifesting itself. I often think about the life of Joseph. (Gen: 37-50) God had given him the vision that all his brothers and even his father, would bow down to him. Joseph's vision did not come to pass until many years later. During this time, he had plenty of opportunity to give up on his vision, but he refused to let go. And when God was ready, the manifestation came. The same is true for David. David was anointed to be king of Israel when he was in his early teens. He did not see the manifestation of the promise of God until he was in his thirties. Like Joseph, David had plenty of opportunities to let go of God's promise, but he found the strength to endure to the end.

These two abovementioned stories show how a stronghold can work to your benefit. A stronghold is a "fortified place" according to Merriam-Weber Dictionary. In other words a stronghold is something that is difficult to remove. In the Old Testament, there is a story in the book of Judges about how the Israelites failed to drive out the inhabitants of the land, as God had instructed them to do. The main reason for their disobedience was because some of the inhabitants of the land refused to relinquish their land. The Nation of Israel was not willing to put forth the extra effort necessary to get the job done. As result, they comprised and allowed the inhabitants to remain in the land. An angel of the LORD eventually came to the people of Israel and rebuked them for their disobedience. He told them that these people, who they allowed to share the land with them, would be a hindrance to them. (Judges 1:27-2:5)

In the same way, we sometimes neglect to walk in the fullness of what God has promised, because we get lazy and comprise with the strongholds in our lives. Your stronghold might be a bad habit, fleshly lust of some kind, or your temper. No matter what it might be, you will never experience the fullness of what God has for your life, until you achieve ultimate victory over that stronghold. In this chapter, I will expose how we will allow strongholds to remain in our lives. With this awareness, you will be in a position not to allow these strongholds to remain; if you chose to do what is necessary to remove them.

First, I would like to introduce a term you might not be familiar with; this term is **"inertia"**. The word inertia comes from the word inert. Inert means too powerless to move. (Merriam- Webster Dictionary 2006) Inertia is commonly used in Thermo-Dynamics to describe an object that should be in motion, but is not. In the context of psychology, this would be the individual who has the answer to his/her problem, but fails to act on the knowledge. For example, I remember sitting on a panel, to determine which inmates would be selected to go into a new pilot program the Sheriff's Department was starting. If the inmate was selected, he would be allowed to be housed in a lower level facility, which means the inmate would have more freedom and more benefits. This particular inmate was very articulate and knowledgeable about drug treatment. He knew all the jargon commonly used in drug treatment. This inmate made quite the impression on some of the panel members. However, I asked him one question: "With all this knowledge you have, why are you still using drugs?" Many of the other panel members wanted to know the answer to my question, too. The inmate paused for a minute and said, "Well, relapse is part of recovery." I then asked the inmate how many times he planned to relapse before he decides to recover. I later pointed out that, according to his file, he had been in recovery mode for almost five years. This is an example on how someone used rationalization to keep the stronghold alive in their life.

I would like to identify some of the most common defense mechanism used to keep an individual in a state of inertia. Sigmund Freud, the founder of Psycho-Dynamic

Theory, identified a number of Defense Mechanisms people sometimes use to protect themselves from change. I will identify ten of the most commonly used defense mechanisms.

Denial: a way of distorting what one thinks or feels in a traumatic situation.

Repression: a means by which painful or threatening thoughts and feelings are excluded from conscious awareness.

Reaction Formation: a way of defending against a threatening impulse by doing the opposite.

Projection: attributing to others, one's own unacceptable desires.

Displacement: a way one discharges impulses from a threatening object to a safer target.

Rationalization: the process of explaining away unacceptable behavior.

Sublimation: the redirection of sexual energy into other channels.

Regression: the process of reverting to a behavior one has outgrown.

Introjection: the process of taking in and assimilating another's values.

Identification: the process in which a person defends against inferiority by identifying with successful causes, people, or organization.

Compensation: a way in which a person masks perceived weaknesses or develops positive traits to make up for limitations.

NOT LETTING GO OF THE PAST

Not letting go of the past can cause you to have a stronghold in your cognitive processes. I have counseled many individuals, who have suffered some kind of traumatic event, who have allowed that event to control their future decisions. Maybe, they were betrayed by a loved one, and now they refuse to let the emotional pain go. So, they go into every relationship with their guard up, so that they will not get hurt again. Or maybe they experienced some other unpleasant circumstance, where they felt threaten in some way. Since that event, they refuse to engage in any activity that reminds them of the prior traumatic event.

It is natural to be apprehensive after experiencing any type of traumatic event. However, we should not allow it to linger for the rest of our lives. This could prove to be detrimental in the long run. Remember, you are responsible for your reactions; don't allow someone or thing to take that control.

IN CONCLUSION

Strongholds can be positive and negative. We must be able to distinguish the difference between the two. When the stronghold is positive it can assist us in maintaining our faith while we wait for the manifestation to come. In the negative, it can hinder us from making positive changes in our lives.

Exercise

Now that you are aware of the commonly used defense mechanisms I want you to list the ones you find yourself using. Be willing to share how you have used this defense mechanism to allow strongholds to remain in your life.

_____, _____, _____,
_____

Out of ten defense mechanisms what if any do you see as being positive? Be ready to explain your answer. _____, _____, _____,
_____ .

FROM THE BEGINNING

In order for us to understand the reason why we need to change our paradigm, we need to understand what took place in the "garden of Eden". I know that many of you have heard the story of how Satan deceived Adam's mate (Eve) into eating from the tree of the knowledge of good and evil. You may have noticed that I used Adam's mate, rather than Eve. The reason why I did this is because when the transgression against God's commandment took place, Eve as we know her now, did not have the name of Eve. She was totally the equal of Adam. When God look down on His creation, He saw them both as equal (Gen 1:28). If you are still doubtful, just keep reading.

Why didn't God just create Eve out of the ground like He did Adam? He could have. The reason He didn't, was because Adam was created a complete being. Adam just was lonely, so God wanted Adam to have someone to fellowship with (Gen 2:18-20). After God created all the animals on the earth; and after Adam named them, there was still no suitable mate for Adam. To remedy the situation, God caused a deep sleep to come over Adam, and He (God) took certain aspects of Adam's being and created a new being (Gen 2:21-25). Think about the traditional wedding vows, "The two shall become one". Where do you think that came from?

When a person gets married to their spouse, it is God's design, they become one whole being. When a person is single, they are not complete. There is something missing. Face it, there are certain things that women by nature are better at than men. Conversely, there are things that men are better at than women. For example according to scientific studies, there are profound differences anatomically, chemically, hormonally, and physiologically in the male and female brain. These differences attribute to the way male and female cognitive processes function. For example, males seem to be highly systemic in their thought process with the ability to compartmentalize information, with a low ability to multitask. Conversely, females seem to have high ability to empathize and multitask with a low ability to compartmentalize. These are just some of the differences that differentiate male and female brains. Please be mindful that there is always an exception to the rule; but, generally speaking, this is true. (www. crosswalk.com/marriage/11568752/)

With the aforementioned in mind, it was God's original plan to have unbroken fellowship with His creation. So, God blessed them (male and female) and instructed them to replenish the earth (Gen 1:28). God wanted a family that He could express His love to. After all God is love (1 John 4:16). What good is love, if you don't have someone or thing to express it to?

However, the enemy of God had another plan in mind. He saw an opportunity to come between man and God. All he had to do was get them (Adam) to disobey God. It is important that you not gloss over this. It is so easy, because we have heard this story so many times. We must understand the ramifications of Adam's disobedience. If you are like me, I always assumed that Adam's mate (Eve) was alone when the transgression occurred. But if you read the scripture carefully you will see that she gave the fruit of the tree of knowledge of good and evil to Adam, who was with her. (Gen 3:6) This is an important aspect to acknowledge, because this will give you insight into our fallen human nature. Why are we so quick to blame others and not take responsibility for our misbehavior? Could it be inherited from Adam? (Gen 3:12)

WHY WAS EATING THE FRUIT SO BAD?

Before the fall, Adam was in a state of innocence. He was ruled by his spirit, and his mind and body were subservient to his spirit. However, if you look at the temptation proposed to Adam, it challenged God's decree. The enemy said, "You will not die.

God knows that you will be able to decide for your self what is good and bad." (Gen 3: 4-5) In essence, you can become your own god. Once Adam took the fruit and ate it, a change occurred. The spirit no longer reigned, and they died spiritually. Now, the mind became ruler and logic reigned in their thought process. Suddenly, they realized that they were naked, because their spiritual clothing was gone. (Gen 3:7) In the New Testament, there is an account of Jesus when he was transfigured. According to the biblical account, his clothes became radiant white. (Mark 9:2-3) I am of the opinion that this was the same clothing that Adam had before the fall.

Now, Adam no longer had to depend on the guidance of God, because he could decide for himself what was right and wrong. He was now like God. Isn't that what caused Lucifer (Satan) to get kicked out of heaven? (Ish 14: 12-14)

WHAT WAS SOME OF THE CONSEQUENCES OF ADAMS TRANSGRESSION?

The first consequence is obvious separation from God. However, there were others too. For one Adam's relationship with his mate changed. Adam was now in a superior position to his mate. We know this because God said that her (Eve) desire would be for her husband, and he would rule over her. (Gen 3:16) As a result, Adam then named his wife Eve. (Gen 3:20) Before then, Adam had no authority to give Eve a name, because they were equal in the eyes of God. However, because he had rule over her, Adam now had the authority give his mate (Eve) a name. In most cultures there still exists a double standard for women, even in so-called modern civilizations like ours. Could it be because of the curse? Praise God that Jesus has redeemed us from the curse and we can function as the curse no longer existed. (Gal 3: 13) But this will not occur unless we renew our minds. (Rom 12:2)

It is important that we not allow traditions to cloud our minds and make the Word of God ineffective in our life. We must search the scriptures and allow the Holy Spirit to bring insight to our minds so that we can change our paradigm to the Christ mind.

WHAT IS MAN?

In this chapter, I would like to discuss the make up of man. When I refer to man, I am speaking in the generic sense, so women don't feel left out. It is my contention that if we don't see ourselves the way God views us, we will never live up to our potential. As I pointed out earlier, God created man in His image and likeness. What does this mean?

First of all, we must understand, that when God formed man out of the earth, He breathed His life into man. (Gen 2:7) That made man different from all the other animals God created, because man had God's spirit in him. It put man into a different class of being. According to scripture, man is described as being a little lower than God. (Psalm 8:4-9) We must understand the position that we hold on the earth, in order to have dominion and control over the challenges that life brings our way. People, who understand this, are the ones who walk in victory.

According to Psalms 82, we will be held responsible for the condition of our world; if, we do not exercise our authority to make this planet a better place to live. Some contend that this scripture refers to angels, but I find that hard to believe. When did God give angels the responsibility to take care of the weak, fatherless, destitute, and afflicted? According to scripture, Angels are ministering spirits sent out to serve on behalf of those who have inherited salvation. (Heb 1:14) We, as believers, have the power to command angels, as long as it is according to God's will. (Psalms 103:20) I know that this statement might be too much for religious minds to handle, but it is scriptural.

Some people find comfort relegating their authority to someone else, because then they can blame others for their problems. But, as we discussed earlier, when we take responsibility for our life, then we put ourselves in a position of control. It is of paramount importance that you realize the potential you possess in order to be what God designed you to be. There are many people who live life far below what God has for them. Some think that this is their plight in life. Others are just ignorant. Which one are you? Well, if you have read this, you can't say you are ignorant anymore. Now, study these scriptures for yourself and allow the Spirit of God to speak to you.

THE MIND ON THREE LEVELS

As a psycho-therapist, I was required to learn a variety of psychological theories. Some of them I found useful and others… One of my favorites was Psycho-Dynamic theory developed by Sigmund Freud. The reason I liked this theory, was because some of the principles coincided with scripture. I made a vow to myself, to only use theories which explained behavior that I can back up with scripture. There are many theories that are good, but if I can't back it up with scripture, I will not use it. With that being said, I like to use the concepts of conscious, subconscious, and unconscious mind. These terms come from the Psycho-Dynamic theory, and I use these terms when I teach classes or clients. I would like to briefly go over each aforementioned to bring you into a deeper understanding how the cognitive process works. I will be using the following explanations:

The Conscious mind- is the part of your mind that makes conscious choices. It is the part of your mind that keeps you in touch with the world you live in. It is our intellect. It was the part of the mind that Adam used to name the animals and plants.

The Subconscious mind- is the part of your mind that controls the conscious mind. It is below the surface. This part of the mind is associated with your personality. It is the part of the mind that makes you unique.

The Unconscious mind- is the most powerful part of the mind, because it controls the subconscious. This is your spirit. Yes, you have a spirit. Even people that are not born again Christians have a spirit. People that are aware of this can achieve great things even though they don't have a relationship with God. This is mentioned in Proverbs 20:27. It states, "The spirit of man is the lamp of the Lord searching all his innermost parts". (ESV)

An analogy that I would like to use to illustrate, how these three components of the mind work together, is an airplane. Most airplanes are equipped with an auto pilot. The function of the auto-pilot is to keep the plane on course once it is in the flight. The pilot is the one responsible for setting the program in order for the auto-pilot to be used. Once the program is set, the plane stays on course. It does not matter how strong the turbulence, it will automatically correct itself, until the pilot disables the system.

Look at the pilot, as your unconscious mind. Its function is to determine what the course is for your life. The subconscious mind would be the auto-pilot, which function is to carry out the directions given by the pilot. The conscious mind would be the actual instruments in the plane that keep the plane on the set course.

WHAT HAPPENED TO THE MIND AFTER THE FALL

It is important to realize what exactly happened to man in the fall. When God said to Adam, "Do not eat from the tree of knowledge of good and evil, or you will die", He was not referring to a physical death. (Gen 2:17) Though physical death eventually occurred; what immediately died was Adam's spiritual link with God. His spirit no longer was in a position of authority. The conscious component of his mind took over. His spirit was placed in submission to the conscious or intellect. Think for a moment about what stops most people from accepting Jesus into their life? What do they say? Most of the time they say something like, "That just does not make sense to me". Or, "I can't believe you would get into that religion stuff. You are too smart for that." The apostle Paul explained it best when he said, "The natural person does not accept the things of God, for it is all folly to him, and they are not able to understand, because they are spiritually discerned" (1Cor2:14)

When a person accepts Jesus as their savior, they are born again spiritually. This means that they have the ability to communicate with God, spiritually. It's like having a radio that receives both AM and FM radio waves. If you turn the switch to receive only AM stations, you will only hear AM stations. However, if you switch to the FM stations, you will be able to hear the FM stations. The same radio has the capacity to receive both radio waves. When a person receives Jesus as their savior, they have the ability to hear the voice of God. They can read scripture and see things that they were not able to see before. They can hear the voice of God talking to them more clearly. They are in a position to know God intimately, and have fellowship with Him.

Unfortunately, our conscious mind and subconscious mind still operate in the same fashion as they did before. That is why we must renew our mind to a new way of thinking. If we don't, then we will be born again, but we will live life like those described in (Psalms 82). We will be like the Christians Paul describes in (1Cor 3:1-3), being fleshly, looking like a mere natural man, living like a natural man. That is not God's plan for you, so why settle for less? God has called you to operate on this planet as a king and priest. (Rev 1:6) This only occurs if you are diligent enough to spend time renewing your mind.

We must reprogram our mind, through the Word of God to create the image of what God has designed us to be. Once that image has been programmed, the unconscious mindset will begin to make it reality. Then the subconscious mind will begin to ensure that you arrive at your destination. Finally, the conscious mind will make the choices you need to make to bring the desire of the unconscious into manifestation. I hope that this explanation is helpful and will motivate you to do the things that are necessary to get you to your promise-land.

THE POWER OF PERCEPTION

Beliefs are the catalyst of every action that we take. Your beliefs dictate your decisions, actions, and behavior. Your beliefs affect the way you perceive the world around you.

To illustrate this point, I want you think about an elephant. Have you ever been to the circus and seen the elephants? When the elephants are not performing, they are usually tied down to a post with a single chain or rope. What keeps that elephant from just pulling that skate up with its trunk? After all, the elephant has more than enough power to do so. The average adult elephant can lift hundreds of pounds with its trunk; surely, it could lift a little wood or metal skate out of the ground.

The reason why the elephant does not do so is because it has been conditioned or trained to think it cannot. You see, when that elephant was a baby it was tied down with a very heavy chain that was attached to a very heavy cement block. When the baby elephant tried to free itself, it was unsuccessful and learned it was futile to try to escape. So, as the elephant grew older, it just resigned itself to the fact it could not free itself from the stake, so why try. It never realized that it had the power to free itself, because it perceived that the task was impossible.

Many of us are just like that elephant. We have allowed our previous experience to condition our thinking. This causes us to be trapped to our past. Many people live mediocre lives because of it. The enemy wants to keep you chained to mediocrity. Why, because you are not a threat. We are not a threat to him when we are in this condition. He says, "Go ahead go to church, read your bible; you can pray and even praise God. I don't care, because you are not going any further than where I allow you to go."

I want you to remember this statement: *What you believe you will perceive, and what you perceive you will act upon.*

COGNITIVE BEHAVIORAL THERAPY

In this chapter I would like to discuss one of my favorite forms of psycho-therapy. I like cognitive behavioral therapy (CBT), because I find the principles of this theory very biblical. The premise of the theory is very simple; your thoughts dictate your behavior. In the book of Proverbs, there is a scripture that encapsulates this theory. "For as a man thinkest in his heart, so is he." (Proverbs 23:7a KJV)

THE THEORY

All forms of Cognitive theory are based on the assumption that our behavior is controlled by our thoughts. According to Dr. Aaron Beck, one of the founders of Cognitive Theory, individual's experience psychological problems when their thought patterns are distorted. To rectify the aforementioned, the thought pattern needs to be replaced or altered. Once this is accomplished the individual will begin to experience a different reality. This is a simplified explanation of the theory.

Some of the cognitive distortions that people commonly use are:

Selective abstractions: taking details out of context and missing the significance of the total picture.

Arbitrary Inference: jumping the conclusion without evidence to support your contention.

Over-generalizations: an unjustified generalization based on a single event.

Polarized thinking: thinking in extremes with no room for the middle ground.

Catastrophizing: anticipation of negative outcomes.

Maximizing/Minimizing: either overestimating the significance of negative events and underestimating the significance of positive events.

Labeling/mislabeling: attaching negative label to a person rather than the behavior.

How many of these distortions have you had recently? If you are honest with yourself, you should be able to identify at least a few of them. If these cognitive distortions are not recognized or addressed, they could lead a person to view the world from a negative and skeptical perspective. This could lead to poor self image and even in some cases depression.

Dysfunctional beliefs have an affect on a person's world view. For example, most people that suffer from depression, is usually because of a negative view of themselves, the world, and their future. They see themselves as unworthy, their environment as hostile, and their future as bleak. It is only when this thought pattern is changed that their outlook will change.

THE WORD OF GOD AS THE AGENT OF CHANGE

There is no better way to change an individual's perspective of themselves than with the Word of God. You can see countless examples of how the Word of God changed people's perspective and caused them to do things that they never thought was possible. For example, the Bible tells us **(63 times)** "fear not", **(37 times)** "be not afraid", and **(28 times)** "by faith". What we find in the Bible is the remedy for the cognitive distortions we may have. That is why it is important to feed on the Word of God everyday. Jesus realized this when he was tempted with hunger in the wilderness. He told the devil that man does not live by bread alone but by the word of God. (Matt 4:4)

We have to develop the same mindset that Jesus had regarding the Word of God. The scriptures can give you the positive affirmations you need to get through tough times. It can change negative beliefs and mental schemas we have learned through our childhood experiences. We must realize that it is our responsibility to renew our thoughts; it does not come automatically. (Rom 12:1-3)

JESUS AND CBT

The bible spoke about Cognitive Behavioral Therapy (CBT) long before the modern day pioneers such as Albert Ellis and Aaron Beck did. In fact, you can find countless examples in both the New and Old Testament where CBT was used. I won't take the time to go over the myriad of examples because I could write an entire book on that subject alone. I will use some examples to illustrate my contention.

One example would be when Jesus was teaching on the Mount of Olive. He told his listeners not to be anxious about their lives. He then proceeded to give examples in nature, like the lilies of the field and the birds. He explained that God takes care of them, so why would you think He (God) would not take care of you. (Matt 6:25-34) What was Jesus' purpose in giving these illustrations? He was attempting to change the people's thoughts about the way they viewed life and God. What is the goal of CBT? To change the way a person thinks about themselves and life.

In the New Testament the apostle Paul wrote a letter to the Church in Philippi. He told them not to be anxious about anything but to submit their cares to the Lord through prayer. He concluded by saying that if you submit your cares to God, His peace would come upon you. (Phil 4:4-13) What was the secret that Apostle Paul was revealing? He was teaching the people to look at their circumstances differently. This is what clinicians call "cognitive restructuring". What most people do not realize is that Paul wrote this while he was incarcerated. Not ideal conditions. He wasn't on some hillside sitting cross legged smelling daisies. He was practicing what he preached.

I hope you see that there are many modern day psychological therapies that evolved from the teachings of the Bible. With this revelation, my faith was strengthened in the relevance of the Bible today. Personally, I found the teaching of the scriptures quite useful in addressing the needs of those who come to me for counsel.

EXERCISE

I would like you to read the account of the spies report on what they found while exploring the Promise Land (Canaan). (Numbers 13:17-33) Once you read this account, answer the following questions:

What did they see?

What was the report of ten of the spies?

Why did the ten spies feel that way?

What was the view of the two spies (Joshua & Caleb)?

Why did they (Joshua & Caleb) feel that way?

You see from this exercise that it is not the environment that has the biggest impact on a person, but rather what they believe about themselves. What you believe, you will perceive, and what you perceive you will act upon. If you don't like your world, change it by changing your beliefs!

RESPONSIBILITY, ACCOUNTABILITY & PURPOSE

Before we continue, there are several concepts or principles that we need to go over. Several years ago I was tasked with the assignment of developing psycho-educational program for juvenile offenders. Though, I was delighted to be given this assignment, I didn't have any idea where to start. I spent time researching all the latest programs that were out there. However, I found those programs to be inadequate. My assessment of those programs turned out to be true, because most of those programs are obsolete.

I then sought the guidance of the LORD. What He revealed to me, were simple concepts or principles. They were responsibility, accountability, and purpose. After these three concepts or principles were introduced to me, I thought about people that I knew that were successful in life. They were highly responsible, they had a sense of accountability, and they had a purpose or goal for their lives. Conversely, people that I knew to be unsuccessful in life had little or no sense of responsibility, little or no sense of accountability, and no definite purpose or goal for their lives.

We, as a society, preach about being responsible, but how many people know what it means? I put this question to the test, by asking various groups of people what it means to be responsible. I was surprised that very few people could answer the question correctly. Then, I realized why so many programs were ineffective, in their efforts to treat and rehabilitate their clients. There is this assumption that everyone has the same concept about responsibility. However, if a person does not have a clear concept of what responsibility means, how can they be responsible? Without a clear concept of what it means to be responsible, there is no motivation to change. If a person is of the belief that their poor choices are attributed to others, then they are reluctant to take responsibility for their choices and are quick to blame others for their actions. They will blame God, their spouse, their parents, their children, the weather etc...

This type of mentality is not conducive to being in control or having dominion over life challenges and circumstances. God created you to have dominion on this earth! (Gen 1:26) This cannot occur with someone who is quick to blame others. So, we must understand the importance of being responsible. A definition I like to use, which is easily understood, is that to be responsible means to be in charge. That means you are responsible for your words, thoughts, actions, and decisions.

Are there influences that will try to capture your will? Most certainly; however, if you recognize the fact that you have final say, and you do not have to allow the influence to control your choices. You can walk away from the influence, and exercise your dominion; as God has designed you to do. For more information on this subject, I invite you to read my book "RAP Therapy for Your Prosperity". In this book I go into more detail on this subject.

ACCOUNTABILITY

The next concept or principle is accountability. Most people get responsibility and accountability confused. Some people think these two principles are the same. Wrong. These two principles go together like peanut butter and jelly, but they are different. The difference between the two is that responsibility causes you to be culpable for the choices or decisions you make, while being accountable causes you to give an account of your actions or choices to someone else. For example, your employer gives you charge of an important assignment. When it is time for that assignment to be completed, the employer will look to you to see if it was done. If the assignment was not done properly, then the employer will want to know why. In other words, the employer wants you to give an account.

People with a strong sense of accountability will consider others before they make choices. We are faced everyday with temptations that we know are not good for us. However, how can we fight those temptations? One way to do it is to think how your actions will impact others. Think about how your loved ones would feel if you made that choice. I am sure Tiger Woods probably would not have been involved in all those extra-martial affairs if he had of thought about the impact it would have on his family.

But that is how temptation works. It causes us to look at the instant gratification and this causes our perspective to be myopic. When we are tempted, we are not thinking about anyone else but ourselves. We are not thinking about the long term ramifications that will occur. Working with offenders in the penal system, I have heard, on numerous occasions, the remorse of making poor choices. Some offenders, are devastated at the hardships they have caused their loved ones because of their poor choices. Many have said, if they would have considered the impact of their decision, they would have made better choices. Once again, I implore you to read "RAP Therapy for Your Prosperity". I go into more detail on this subject.

PURPOSE

The last principle or concept will be purpose. There are many words that are synonymous with purpose. For example, reason, goal, mission, objective, etc. Purpose is vital in motivation. Without a sense of purpose or reason, there is no motivation. The more the sense of purpose you have, the more the sense of motivation or urgency. Sports teams that excel are the teams that have created a sense of purpose for winning. This year's NFL Super bowl Champions used the city of New Orleans as one of their reasons for wanting to win the championship. What separates teams that are virtually the same in talent? It is the team that generates the higher degree of purpose that will prevail.

Having a sense of purpose, gives us a sense of focus. With this sense of focus, we can ignore the distractions that are designed to detour us from the path of success. When the times of trial comes our way, we can run right through it if we remind ourselves of what our objective is. Jesus used this throughout the gospels when he said, "I come to do the will of my father." (John 4:34) We must remember that Jesus functioned in a human body and was prone to many of the temptations we are subject to. He experienced hunger, frustration, anger, and fatigue just like us. But, he was able to overcome these temptations, because he reminded himself of why he was here and what he needed to accomplish.

We, too, need to remind ourselves of why we are here, and what we need to accomplish. Many people have no real sense of purpose, other than living a comfortable life. Quite often, I will ask my clients, "What is your purpose in life?" Unfortunately, some of them cannot give me an answer. These are usually the individuals with the most issues. Having a sense of purpose will give you fulfillment in your life, because you have a reason to get up in the morning. You have something to strive for, and you greet everyday with expectation no matter what the circumstance you find yourself in. One of the common characteristics of depression is a sense of hopelessness. (DSM IV Desk Reference pg 174, 2002). People that are hopeless usually do not have a positive outlook on life.

So, it is of paramount importance, to cultivate a sense of purpose for your life. A sense of purpose will cause you to keep focused. It will provide motivation when the trials tribulations come your way. It will generate a sense of expectancy and keeps you hopeful and less prone to depression. So, I strongly recommend that you ask yourself, "What is my purpose for being on this earth?" If you cannot come up with an answer that is alright, I am sure with God's help you will find an answer to this question.

IN CONCLUSION

Understanding the importance of responsibility causes individuals to take control or charge of their choices or actions. When this occurs, they are less likely to blame others for their poor choices and behavior. This in turn causes them to be more amiable to correction.

Understanding the importance of accountability causes the individual to consider others before they make choices. Many times people make poor choices because they are consumed with their own self interest. They are enticed with their own desires and are led down the path of deception, which ultimately leads to destruction.

Understanding the importance of purpose causes the individual to remain focused. This focus will generate a sense of motivation that is necessary to endure hardships. It also provides a sense of expectancy that causes a person to be excited and energized when others are just going through the motions.

THE FAITH OF ABRAHAM

One morning I awoke to a revelation about faith. I immediately went to my Bible and read Romans 4:13-25. What was described in those scriptures was the kind of faith Abraham had to receive the promise God had given him. Think for a moment the circumstances Abraham was in. First of all, God was leading him to a land he had never been before. (Gen 12:1) He (Abraham) was separated from his support group. Finally, God had told him that he would have a child, even though his wife was barren. (Gen 15:4) Talk about impossible circumstances! Imagine how hard it must have been for him, to believe God. I know doubt was knocking at his door every time he would rehearse the promise God gave him in his mind. How did Abraham prevail?

I will give you a strategy to use when you find yourself in a similar situation. First of all, you need to realize that if God has promised you something, He will fulfill His promise to you. You must remind yourself that God is incapable of lying to you. (Num 23:19)

In the book of Genesis chapter 15, the bible gives the account of God making a covenant with Abraham. The reason why God did this was to reinforce His commitment to fulfill His promise. Abraham did not have the Bible like we do. So, God did something that Abraham could understand. He made a blood covenant with Abraham. The blood covenant was significant in those days, because it meant that if you did not fulfill your obligation, you placed a curse upon yourself and your family. The blood covenant was the highest form commitment that a person could make.

God made that covenant with Abraham to ensure him that He would do what He had promised. Today, we have the Word of God, which contains the promises God has made to us as believers. Once we realize that God's promises apply to us like it did to Abraham, then we can function in the same manner as Abraham did. (Gal 3:26-29) We can rely on the Word of God just like Abraham did.

When this revelation came to me, I understood what the scripture meant when it said," Abraham hoped against hope in believing God's promise to him, that he would be the father of many nations". (Rom 4:18) I understood how he could ignore his physical condition and the condition of his wife; (Rom 4:19) and finally, how he could fight against the doubt that attempted to rob him of his faith. (Rom 4:20) He did it by standing on the covenant God had made with him. We must do the same thing.

We must go to the Word of God and stand on the promises God has made to us. We must fight the enemy with the Word of God, when he comes to rob us, of what we believed God for. (Eph 6:10-17) We must be able to look beyond the seemingly insurmountable circumstances we find ourselves in and just stand on the Promise God has given us.

Has God given you a promise that you thought was impossible? Has he given you a vision or dream that you refused to act upon because you thought that it was too great for you to accomplish? Have you allowed fear to keep you discouraged and at a stay still? If this is true, then you must do what God instructed Joshua to do. You must meditate on the Word of God, speak those words, and finally act on what you have read and meditated on. (Joshua 1:6-9) If you will do this, then you will enter your promise land. Now, go out and claim the land that God has given you!

THE FORCE OF FAITH

In order for us to achieve our dreams, we must understand what faith is. Since, we are created in the image and likeness of God; we can operate in this world, in the same manner as He (God) operates in the Universe. I am not saying we are God, but what I am saying is that we are in the God class. (Psalms 82:6)

With this knowledge, we can use the force of faith to create what we desire. According to the scriptures God created the heavens and earth by faith. (Heb 11:3) The scriptures also states, that it is impossible to please God without faith. (Heb 11:6) What causes God to act on your behalf is your faith. Not your tears, your pain, or your feelings. It is your faith. Many people are under the impression that if they just cry out to God in despair, it will cause Him to come to their rescue. This might work for someone that is new in the faith, because of God's grace. However, God expects you to grow in maturity; so that you no longer have to constantly rely on His grace.

What you need to realize is that you have a responsibility to understand the dynamics of faith and to use that faith to activate God to act in your behalf. Look at your faith as spiritual money, which you use to purchase what you want in this physical earth.

YOU MAY TO NEED TO RECHARGE THE BATTERY

Once we release our faith through our words, we need to understand that what we asked for is not going to happen right away. Sometimes, it may take days, weeks, months, and even years to manifest. What do we do in the meantime? You need to understand that your faith may become weak and in some cases diminish all together. Because there is an enemy out there that wants to discourage you. You also have a world that can present challenges to you, and finally your natural mind, that does not understand the things of the spirit.

This is where having a positive support system can assist you. Your support system may be members from your family, friends, counselor, or clergy. It could also be positive affirmations that you say to yourself, or a (dream wall) that you created. I personally like to read bible scriptures pertaining to what I have released my faith for. When the doubt comes, I fight back by reminding myself who I am, and what I can do because of it. That is why it is vital to read your bible, and keep in prayer daily. This will keep your faith fully charged until the manifestation comes to pass in your life.

TRUST THE PROCESS YOU AREN'T READY YET

If you are like me you have questioned why God did not answer your prayer when you thought He should. I have had people prophesize over me, with the great things God had in store for me. However, years later that prophecy hadn't come to past. Why? Could it be that they were wrong or misinformed? Could it be that God was lying to them? Or, could it be that the promise was conditional, and I did not fulfill my part of the obligation. In most cases the latter is true. We must realize that all of the promises of God come with a condition of some kind. For example, Abram had to separate himself from his family before God would bless him. (Gen 12: 1-3) If Abram had not obeyed God instruction, he would have never received the blessing. In the book of Isaiah it states that if you are willing and obedient you will eat the good of the land. (Ish 1:19)

It is important for us to realize that we have a part to play in obtaining God's blessings for our lives. It does not happen automatically. It's not going to happen just because you get excited and jump up and down, and say Praise God at the top of your lungs. It will happen when you obey the instructions that God has given you through His Spirit: His Word, or the person He has designated to instruct you.

When I was in grad school, I had a professor who constantly told us just to, "Trust the process" and we would get through school. Sometimes, I have to admit, I was overwhelmed with all the homework and studies. But, three years later, I graduated. I often look back with fondness about the experience I had with my fellow graduate students- How we would complain about the amount of work we had to do. It was like being in an academic boot camp for three years. But now, I am grateful for the experience.

In the same way, the Spirit of God can prepare you for what God has assigned for you. We must trust God that He will complete what He promised us; if we will do our part. I would have never graduated, if I did not follow the instructions of my professors. Likewise, we must commit ourselves to following the guidance of the LORD, if we are to achieve what He desires us to achieve. I was reading one of my favorite scriptures in the book of Jeremiah. It says, "Blessed is the man that trust in God for he will be like a tree planted by the water. It will not fear when the heat comes nor will be afraid in the year of a drought, but it will continue to produce its fruit without ceasing". (Jer17:7-8) One day, the Spirit of the LORD told me to continue reading the next two verses.

What I saw was why God will delay our blessings. It is to teach us. It is to show us what is in our heart. Sometimes we think we are ready for something, but in reality we are not. God would be doing us a disservice, if He gave us what we wanted, when we thought we wanted it. I can think back on times when God had promised me something; and I was glad that He did not give it to me, because I was not ready for it.

It would be like giving a two year old the keys to your car, because they wanted to drive it. How many parents would do that? That child does not have the capabilities to operate that vehicle. Not only would their life be in danger, but anyone that happened to be on the road, or in the car with them. In the same way, many of us are like children in our walk with God. We have not taken the time to grow spiritually. It doesn't matter how long you have been going to church. What matters is how much time you spend in the presence of God, studying His Word. It matters how much time you spend at the feet of the Holy Spirit, in prayer and mediation. Once God can trust you, then He will allow His blessings to flow in your life. You have to qualify before the blessings come. What has God called you to do that you have neglected? How much time do you spend in His presence? How obedient are you to His instructions? Maybe this is the reason, why you haven't seen the manifestation of God's promises in your life.

TWO KINDS OF FAITH

As I was studying the Word of God, the thought came to me about faith. I suddenly felt led to read several scriptures on the subject. After reading these scriptures, a deep revelation about faith came to me. It amazes me how alive the Word of God is! You can read the same scripture a thousand times and get a different meaning every time you read it. This was my experience when I read the story about Peter getting out of the boat at the command of Jesus. I had read this story at least a hundred times; but, this time The Holy Spirit showed me something that I had not considered before. What was revealed to me was the concept of having different levels of faith.

What do I mean? What I realized is that we can operate in a faith that is based in human logic, or we can operate in the God kind of faith. Most people, including "some Christians", operate in the former rather than the latter. The reason for this is that we have been conditioned to rely on our intellect (conscious mind), rather than our spiritual mind (unconscious mind).

We have been trained from birth, to develop our cognitive processes in order to function in this world. We have been indoctrinated, through the educational system, to base our decisions of empirical evidence. We have been taught that if something cannot be empirically tested, it is not valid. That is why it is written in the scriptures that the natural man cannot accept the things of God, because they are foolishness to him. (1Cor 2:14) The natural man bases his knowledge on those things, which he/she can understand from a logically perspective or by their senses. However, the Spiritual man is not limited to just logical understanding.

The individual, who has the Spirit of God within them, has the capability to operate in the realm of the spirit. In this realm, where God resides, nothing is impossible! Many believers have mistakenly thought their faith was based on God, when in reality, it was not. It was based on their logical understanding, clothed as faith in God. I call this type of faith natural faith.

Christians are not the only people capable of using faith. There are people who never read the bible, who have achieved great things because of their use of faith. What we must realize is that the principles of God will work for anyone who uses it. You can go to any book store and find volumes of books about positive thinking. All these books are based on some concept(s) from the scriptures. They just have been repackaged and secularized to make it more appealing to the general population. With this being said, I want to briefly describe what natural faith is and compare it with the God kind of faith.

NATURAL FAITH

As I previously stated, natural faith is based in the sense realm. It operates from our logic and past experiences. For example, when you get into your car, you have faith that it will start and take you where you want to go. The only exception would be, if you were aware of some type of malfunction in the vehicle which would cause it not to start all the time. Where did you get the faith to know that your vehicle would start? Was it based on your previous experiences, knowledge and observations? All of the aforementioned are based on either logic or the senses. This is what I call natural faith.

The problem with natural faith is that it is fallible. This means that because it is based on the natural, it can fail. Have you ever exercised your faith for something and it did not happen? Did you rationalize that maybe God did not want you to have it? Maybe, you thought you did not pray hard enough, or fast long enough, to get God's attention.

I submit to you, that maybe it was not any of the aforementioned; rather, you were operating in natural faith and not the God kind of faith.

THE GOD KIND OF FAITH

The God kind of faith is based on God and His Word exclusively. It is not limited by human logic or the senses. (1Cor 2:15) From scripture, we understand that God created the world by faith. (Heb 11:3) We also know that it is impossible to please God without faith. (Heb 11:6) God is not moved by anything else but faith! He is not moved by your tears or pain. There are many people under the assumption that if they cry long enough or hard enough, that God will answer their prayers. Then they get frustrated and mad at God when their prayers go unanswered.

There are many people who have turned away from following God, because of the abovementioned. There are many believers who are bitter and have resigned themselves not to operate in faith, because they do not understand the concepts of what I am sharing with you now. These individuals are quick to discourage anyone who dares to venture out in faith by relating what happened to them when they attempted to walk in faith.

The first thing to know, when you are operating in the God kind of faith, is that it will not fail. It will not fail because God cannot fail. This type of faith is based on God and Him alone. When you operate in this type of faith, you do not need to rely on the intellect (conscious mind). In fact, when you operate in this kind of faith, your logic will attempt to hinder you, because it wants some empirical evidence. You must realize this, because that is how the conscious mind has been trained. When you first step out in the God kind of faith, it is natural for you to have doubt in your mind.

There is a difference between in having doubt in your mind, and having it in your heart. As I discussed earlier, the heart refers to the inner man; or your human spirit. The mind refers to conscious mind or the intellect. When Peter asked Jesus, how he was able to curse the fig tree; and have it withered the next day, Jesus told him it was because he had faith, and did not doubt in his heart. (Mark 11:23) Noticed he did not say doubt in your mind, but in the heart.

Another mistake commonly made when a person steps out in faith, is that they have faith in their faith, rather than having faith based on the person of God. There are a myriad of people who have achieved great things, because they had faith in their faith. However, this type of faith is fallible. That is why when Jesus revealed to Peter how he was able to successfully curse the fig tree, he started out by saying have faith in God or have the God kind of faith.

When you have the God kind of faith, you have the assurance that whatever you ask for will come to pass. (John 14:14, 15:7) This type of faith will give you the confidence to speak to your mountain and know that it will obey you, because it is not based on your ability or your faith but God's faith. From the scriptures, we know what God has promised will come to pass, because it is impossible for God to lie. (Heb 6:18)

Once you understand this type of faith and begin to operate in this realm, it will become easier. Eventually, you will experience less resistance, from your conscious mind; because it will have past experiences to refer to. Jesus never operated in any other kind of faith. Well, we can learn to operate in this realm, as well. Soon, you will be operating in the God kind of faith and others will marvel at how confident you are; that whatever you ask for will come to pass. This will occur because you know that your faith is not based in yourself, but in the Power of God; because nothing is impossible with Him. (Luke 1:37)

You will be like the tree Jeremiah spoke of, that is planted by the waters, who does not fear; when the heat comes or is afraid in the year of drought, because its faith is in the Lord and of the Lord. (Jer 17:7-8)

PETER WALKS ON THE WATER

In closing this chapter, I would like to give you an example of how a person can start out in the God kind of faith, but revert back to a natural type of faith. The example I would like to use is from Matt 14:27-33. In this story, Jesus had commanded his disciples to go ahead of him in the boat, while he dismissed the people who had come to listen to him teach. After dismissing them, Jesus went to an isolated place to pray.

When Jesus had finished praying, he went to meet his disciples. Because of the strong winds, the disciples were having difficulties crossing the sea. Between the hours of 3:00AM-6:00AM, Jesus approached the disciples walking on the water. When the disciples saw him, they thought he was a ghost, and began to scream. What would you think if you saw someone walking on the water at 3:00AM?

When Jesus heard the disciples scream, he assured them that he was not a ghost. Hearing Jesus, Peter decided to test Jesus contention. Peter said, "If it is really you, then permit me to come to you". Jesus told him to come. With that, Peter immediately got out of the boat and began to walk towards Jesus. At that moment, he was operating in the God kind of faith. However, it did not last; because when Peter started looking at how hard the wind was blowing, his logic (conscious mind) overrode his inner man (unconscious mind). When this happened, he started to panic; and fear set in. When the fear set in, Peter's faith disappeared; because faith and fear are total opposites. Just like day and night cannot exist at the same time, neither can faith and fear exist at the same time.

When the fear set in and Peter began to sink, Jesus was close enough for him to grab Peter. Once they got to the boat, Jesus rebuked Peter for having little faith. What can we learn from this story? There are many things; but what I want to focus on, is the importance of not allowing external circumstances to dictate our faith. When we do this, we are like Peter, who looked at the wind instead of keeping his mind on the word of Jesus.

When we step out in faith, based on something that God has promised us, we need not look for anything else to validate our faith. When we do this, we give opportunity for doubt and fear to come in and rob us of our faith. People, who operate in the God kind of faith, have trained themselves, not to look at their circumstances. The only validation they need is the Word of God.

Another lesson to be learned is what to do when you find yourself beginning to doubt. When this occurs, you need to put your focus back on the Word or Promise God has given you. Just like Peter, we sometimes begin in faith; but allow our conscious mind to take over, because what we are experiencing is contrary to what we have released our faith for. If this thought process goes unabated for too long, fear will manifest itself and rob you of operating in faith. So, you must be aware when this happens and stop it. You stop it by reminding yourself, of the promises of God and His Word. When you do this, Jesus will come and grab you to make sure you don't sink; just in the same way he grabbed Peter. Because Jesus is the same today as he was back then. (Heb 13:8) I hope that this has assisted you in becoming more aware of the two kinds of faith and developing a strategy to become more skilled in operating in the God kind of faith.

THE POWER PRINCIPLES OF (WORKING) FAITH

This chapter will focus on how you can get your faith to work for you. In order for this to happen, you need to be aware of some things. When I first came to know the LORD, it was during the Charismatic renewal in the eighties. I witnessed and experienced the LORD use people for great deliverances. Unfortunately, there were some, who allowed their flesh to get in the way. This caused this powerful movement of God to have a bad reputation in some circles. Some people called preachers like Kenneth Copeland, Fred Price and Charles Capps "the name it and claim it bunch". This group of preachers taught on the power of your words and faith. In some religious circles, they were maligned and ridiculed for their beliefs. Because of this, many believers discredited their teachings. Fortunately, I was not one of them.

I knew in my spirit what these men of God were teaching was true. I could see it in their lives and life style. I knew that I wanted the same relationship they had with God. I wanted the benefits which come with that kind of relationship. Now, twenty something years later, I am experiencing it. Hopefully, it will not take you that long. I would like to share with you some principles that will assist you in living the kind of life God has for you.

THE POWER OF BELIEF

In order for faith to work, you have to have belief. Belief is the catalyst of our actions. This is what makes beliefs so powerful. Your beliefs determine how you respond to situations. Beliefs can influence the way you perceive situations, and this perception can dictate the way you respond. What I teach is *"What you believe you will perceive. What you perceive you will act upon."* If you view a person or situation as adversarial, then you will react with fear and distrust. If you view the same person as an ally, you will respond differently. Even though, the actions of the aforementioned were the same. Why? It is because you perceived their actions differently, because of your beliefs.

Let me give you an example of what I am talking about. Recently, I was asked to sit on a panel because a student felt she was not treated fairly by her teacher. It was the contention of this student that the teacher was showing favoritism to one student, and she was being discriminated against. It appeared this student had an issue with another student in the class. She felt the teacher did not handle the situation properly. The student was so upset about the alleged mishandling that she refused to complete the final project for the class. Her belief was if the teacher had handled the situation properly, she would not have been upset and would have been emotionally prepared to take the final exam.

Well, it turned out that the student's grade was not determined because of her failure to complete the final for the class. In fact, she was given full credit for the final by the teacher. The real reason she received the grade was because of her prior test scores.

There are many directions I could go with the abovementioned scenario, but I want to stay with the power of belief. This student allowed her belief about being discriminated against to control her emotions; to the point she was emotionally unable to do her assignment. I took this opportunity to point this out to the student. She realized that she allowed someone else's behavior to control her decisions, giving them power over her. Now, she is the one who suffered the consequences, of that choice. We must not minimize the power of beliefs, and understand the dynamics of beliefs.

BELIEVING AND MENTALLY ASSENTING

I find many people do not understand the difference of believing and mentally assenting to something. The main difference between the two is commitment. A person can mentally agree with something in principle but never act on what they mentally assent to. For example, a person says they believe in the sanctity of marriage but later get caught in an adulterous affair. Did that person really believe what they profess on the marriage alter, or were they mentally assenting to the principle? If they really believed, then the adulterous affair would not have occurred.

Unfortunately, we live in an age of mental assenters. That is why there is so little power in the church today. The church for the most part, is the living example of what the apostle Paul described in (2 Tim 3:5). Having a form of godliness, but not demonstrating the power. I know some of you might not like what I said and might be offended, but someone has to tell you the truth. If you are offended, get over it.

We must question ourselves, whether we truly believe the Word of God, or are we assenting to it. It is only when we answer this question we can move to the next level. The life of Abraham is an excellent example of the act of believing. The bible describes a situation, where God called Abraham to leave his country and family, to go to a land he had never been before. God promised Abraham, that He would bless him. (Gen 12:1-3)

Abraham demonstrated his belief by acting in faith and leaving his country. As a result, God was able to bless Abraham with livestock, silver and gold. (Gen 13:2). In fact, God bless Abraham with so much that Abraham and his nephew (Lot) had to separate, because the land could not contain them both. (Gen 13:5-12)

God is looking for people that will take him at His Word and demonstrate the same kind of faith that Abraham had. People who are not willing to let their feeling or emotions discourage them. People, who will not allow the circumstances, dictate their reactions-people who will allow the Word of God, to have final authority, in their lives. I implore you to read (Rom 4:13-25) there you will find what is necessary for you to have the faith that pleases God.

THE DYNAMICS OF FAITH

In order to have the power of God demonstrated in your life, you need to understand the dynamics of faith. From the bible, we understand it was by faith, through the word of God that the universe was created. (Heb 11:4) From the scriptures, we understand it is impossible to please God without faith. (Heb 11:6) So, it behooves us to have and understand faith.

Faith is a spiritual substance that is not detected by the physical senses. But, you can see the effects of faith in the physical world. Faith is like the wind; you cannot see the wind, but you can see the effects of the wind. Faith operates in the same manner.

There was a situation when Jesus was teaching in a town. The house was packed. It was standing room only. There were these four men, who wanted to bring their friend in, so Jesus could heal him. No one would let them in, so they climbed up on the roof, opened a hole in the roof, and let their friend down in front of Jesus. There are many messages in this story, but what I want to focus on, is what the scriptures said when Jesus saw these men's actions. It states that **Jesus saw their faith**. (Mark 2:5) This is important to remember. These men demonstrated their faith, with their actions. They were committed, and demonstrated that commitment by climbing up on the roof and letting their friend down on a rope to Jesus. Because of this, Jesus responded by healing the man. (Mark 2:12)

James, Jesus brother, put it this way. Faith without actions is dead. (James 2:17) There are many people who talk of having faith, but their actions are not congruent with what they profess. They are mental assenters. Their talk sounds good, but their actions are wanting. If you want God to move in your behalf, you must make up your mind, to put some action to your faith. Otherwise, you are only deceiving yourself and playing games with God.

WORDS AND FAITH

Once you come to understand the power of belief and faith, the next thing you need to understand is the power of your words. Words are powerful, because they are the containers of our thoughts. Words paint pictures and create images in our unconscious mind. Words are seeds, that when planted in our unconscious mind, create a harvest in our physical experience.

When a person realizes this, they will scrutinize their words. Jesus spoke on many occasions about the power of words. In one situation he stated, "If you believe in your heart and do not doubt what you say, it will be done." (Mark 11:23)

Our words release our faith. In the same way God created the universe, we can create the environment we live in. God created an image in his mind, believed it would happen, and released his faith through His Word. In the book of John, it states, that in the beginning was the Word. It further states, that the Word was with God, and all things were created through this Word. (John1:1-3) If you don't like your world; I invite you to examine your words. The problem might be right under your nose.

In conclusion, I would like to end this chapter by asking you a few questions.

What are some areas where you have been guilty of mentally assenting rather than believing?

What are some things that you have strong beliefs in? How would I know that you have strong belief in this area?

Are your words and actions congruent with what you profess to believe?

What makes Abraham's faith different from yours?

If you answer these questions truthfully you will be able to assess where you are and plan a strategy to get you to the next level. Please remember it is not where you start, but where you end that matters.

THE FAITH OF THE CENTURION

I felt impressed, to write about the faith of the centurion, because of the comment Jesus made about this man and his faith. According to the scriptures, it says Jesus marveled at this man's faith. He said that no one in Israel had his kind of faith. (Matt 8:10) What made this man's faith so unique that Jesus would make this comment? If we can learn this, then we can have Jesus say the same thing about us.

What we know about the centurion is that he was a God fearing man. This means, even though he was outside of the covenant, he believed in the teachings of God. He probably came to his belief because of the testimony of his servant(s). This can be seen in the fact that when he approached Jesus, because his servant was ill. (Matt 8:5-6) When Jesus said he would come to his home, the man immediately said that Jesus did not need to come to his house; all he had to do was speak the words of healing. (Matt 8:8)

What did this man know that others did not know? Here lies the secret of releasing your faith and exercising your authority on this earth.

First, you must realize who is the resource of your power. You must acknowledge God as your source and no one else. Your job is not your source, your business is not your source, and the world economy is not your source. **God is your source**.

Second, you must understand the importance of authority and having a sense of protocol. With everything in life, there is order. This makes everything run smoothly and less chaotic. When an individual knows their place, whether it be in the family or business setting, there is less friction. Why do you think one of the Ten Commandments states, "Honor your father and mother, so that your days will be long on the earth" (Due 5:16). Most interpersonal problems begin when there is schism, and the parties start to question the leadership.

Third, when you submit to the leadership above you, and prove yourself faithful in following instructions, you are in a position to be trusted with more responsibility.

Because the centurion knew these principles, he was promoted to lead a company of 100 men. He knew, just like he follows the orders of those who are above him, he could expect the same behavior from those that were under him. He knew that there would be consequences for those who would deliberately disobey the orders given by a superior commander. The centurion just applied these same principles to Jesus. He understood, if Jesus commanded healing to come to his servant, then it would happen. The centurion knew Jesus was under the authority of God, just like he was under the authority of his superior commanders. With obedience comes confidence to ask and receive.

Jesus made this clear when he said, "If you abide in me, and my words abide in you, ask whatever you wish, and it will be done for you."(John 15:7 ESV) When we submit ourselves to the Word of God and its authority, we can be trusted to carry out God's will on this earth. With this obedience comes blessings or rewards.

It is to our benefit to humble ourselves and not allow our intellect to rule our lives totally. This world system promotes this mindset. This post-modernistic world we live in, tells us that there are many avenues to get to God. It tells us, that we can be our own god, and all we need to do is reach a certain level of enlightenment. It sounds good, but didn't the enemy sound good to Eve in the garden? (Gen 3:6)

Take advantage of what God has done for you through this son Jesus. Your spirit has been restored in order that through the renewing of your mind you can walk in harmony with God like Adam did before the fall, and like Jesus did, while he was on this earth. But, in order for this to happen, you have to break the strongholds which keep you bound to being ordinary. God did not create you to be ordinary. In fact, He dislikes ordinary (Rev 3:15-16). I don't know about you, but I don't want God to spit me out of His mouth, because I was not motivated enough to take advantage of what He made available to me.

I encourage you to ponder, on these subjects that I covered. I know for some of you this subject matter was hard to digest. Just keep chewing on it, and eventually you will be able to digest it and put these teaching into practice in your life. Hopefully, it won't take as long as it took me. No matter how long it takes, know that you will get to your promise land. Be strong in the Lord and the Power of His might.

WHO DO YOU TRUST (MAMMON OR GOD)?

In this chapter, I am going to bring up the subject of money. I know this is a sensitive subject to discuss. If you are like me, when I hear the subject brought up in the context of church, my guard goes up. I put on the shades of skepticism, and see visions of preachers spending their parishioner's hard earned money inappropriately. To be honest, it was not until recently, that I grasped the true understanding on giving. Now, I have peace when I give. I would like to share what the Holy Spirit taught me.

GOD'S PURPOSE OF WEALTH

The reason why God wants his people to have wealth and prosper is to show the world what He is willing to do for those who place their trust in Him. When a child of God is prosperous, it is a testimony to the goodness of God. If we realize that God wants us to be prosperous and enjoy the finer things in life, then we unlock the door for the provision of God to enter into our lives. The problem with most people is that they have been led to believe that it is "worldly" to have an abundance of possessions. It is worldly to sit in first class while traveling. It is worldly, to live in an upper class neighborhood. With this mindset, you will not allow yourself to pursue wealth and feel guilty if you obtained it.

We must remember that God has given us the power to obtain wealth to establish his covenant on this earth. (Due 8:18) If we understand that God is our source and the purpose of our being prosperous is not just for our personal satisfaction but to be a conduit of blessings to others, then where is the problem? What kind of testimony would a person have if they can't pay their bills, and when someone is in need, all they can do is pray for them? How attractive is that to a person who does not know the Lord?

I will give you an example of what I am talking about. I was attending a church service and during the service a young man came to the alter in tears because he was informed by his doctor that he would need surgery. The problem was that the young man did not have medical insurance to cover the surgery. No one in the church had the money to pay for this man's surgery. All they could do is lay hands on him and anoint him with oil. Now, I am not against either praying or laying of hands on someone, however, if the person's faith is not at a level to receive, it is for not. It would have been nice if someone said, "I will pay for that surgery." This is what I am talking about, being a blessing to someone. Imagine the testimony that young man would have, of the glory of God, if someone would have offered to pay for his surgery. What better testimony is there?

TITHING VS GIVING

I often asked myself the question, is the tithe valid for the New Testament believers? There are some that say that it is and others who disagree. I am not here to advocate for either side. The one thing I know, it is God's will that we share our blessings with others. From the scriptures, I understand that God blessed Abram in order that he may be a blessing to others. (Gen 12:1-3) Since I am heir to the promise of Abraham, (Gal 3:26-29) then I am entitled to everything that God promised Abraham.

Now with that blessing comes a responsibility. The responsibility is not just to be blessed for my personal benefit but use it to be a blessing to others. As I do this, I will be a conduit for God to funnel His blessings into the earth. It is just that simple. With this understanding it does not matter how much I give or when I give. All that matters is that I am obedient to His voice.

I find many churches will use strategies to manipulate people to give their money.

Many do it because they fear that if they don't use such tactics, they won't be able to meet their budgets. The sad thing is that many of these churches don't meet their budgets, because they allow the spirit of fear to control their thoughts. Faith and fear cannot operate together. You will either submit to one or the other.

According to scripture God loves a cheerful giver. (2Cor 9:7) How can someone give cheerfully if they feel they are being manipulated or pressured? If that individual does give, they will probably not see the reward. Because usually there is not faith attached to the gift, which means there is no expectation of reward. So what eventually happens? This person will either quit giving or just start tipping God when it is convenient to do so.

Instead, if a person understands the principles of giving, they will be more incline to give and will be happy about it. Why? Because they understand the reason why they are to give and know that God will bless them. (Luke 6:38) One of the most misunderstood scriptures used to manipulate people to give is found in (2Cor 9:6-8). The reason I say this is because it's quite often used out of context. In order to get the real meaning of the aforementioned scripture, you need to read the entire eighth chapter. The apostle Paul, was commenting of how some of the believers were giving more than their share to compensate for those who could not give. He encouraged them to continue in their giving, because God would bless them for it. Once you understand this, then (2Cor 9:6-13) makes sense. In essence, what the apostle was saying is, those of you who give much will receive much in return, and those of you that give little will get little in return; for you're giving. The bottom line is you will receive a return on the proportion of your giving.

For example, a person takes a handful of corn seeds, and plants them in the ground. What is their expectation going to be? Now another person plants a bag of corn seed into the ground. What is their expectation going to be, when the harvest time comes? It would be foolish, for the person who planted the handful of seeds, to be upset because they did not receive the same harvest that the person who planted the bag of seeds.

Once I grasped this truth, I understood that the more I give, the more I would receive in return from God. Giving was no longer a problem. In fact, I look forward to giving, because I know that it is pleasing to God; and He will reward me for my obedience to Him.

DON'T EAT YOUR SEED

Now, I would like to share another truth that I learned to increase your financial harvest. This concept I found in the scriptures. *He who supplies seed to the sower and bread for food will supply and multiply your seed for sowing and increase the harvest, you will be enriched in every way for all the generosity, which through us will produce thanksgiving to God. (2Cor 9:10-11 ESV)*

The apostle Paul was encouraging the believers to continue in their giving even though some of them were giving more than others. Based on this, he (Apostle Paul) made the abovementioned statement. What does it mean? The principle is this: if a person gives more, then they will receive more. The person who gives less will receive less. But there is another principle too. The principle is, if you ask God for seed he will provide it for you.

What most people do when they get the seed, they will spend it on something other than sowing. For example, lets say a person is blessed with an extra $100.00. At that point, they have a choice to either take a portion of that money and sow it, or spend it on themselves. If they chose the latter, they ate their seed and their harvest will not increase. If they chose the former, they will increase their harvest, because they have more seed to plant. If a person uses this principle, they will increase their harvest. The larger your harvest the more seed you have to plant. The more seed you have to plant the bigger your harvest… Get the picture. So, a person could start out with very little seed to plant, and through this process, increase their seed potential. Before they know it, they will have plenty of seed to plant, because their harvest is greater. In essence, as God blesses them, they in turn are in a position to be a bigger blessing to others. This is the principle of "sowing and reaping". It works, trust me. But I implore you, when you get blessed with extra income don't eat your seed! Take a portion of that seed and plant it, so that you can receive a larger harvest.

PLANT WITH AN EXPECTATION TO RECEIVE

Many believers that give do not attach any expectation on their seed. They just throw it in the offering basket with little expectation. For many people, giving an offering or tithe is little more than a ritual. With this attitude, there is not enough faith to make any thing happen for them. Giving becomes more of drudgery than a pleasure. If this is you, then I want you to do two things. First, I want you to read (Mark 10: 17-31). Then after you do that, I want you to do an experiment. I want you to write down every time you give money to the benefit of others. When you give this money, I want you to believe that God is going to increase whatever you have given ten times. In other words, if you give $20.00, believe God will give you back $200.00. When it comes, don't eat your seed. Instead, next time give $40-50.00, and continue this process. Eventually, you will be able to give $1000.00; and you know what the return on that is. I hope, this chapter encourages you to start getting involved in God's system of finance. It works trust me!

""Americans who earn less than $10,000 gave 2.3 percent of their income to religious organizations," Smith, Emerson, and Snell write, "whereas those who earn $70,000 or more gave only 1.2 percent." While the actual percentages are slightly higher for Christians who regularly attend church, the pattern is similar. Households of committed Christians making less than $12,500 per year give away roughly 7 percent of their income, a figure no other income bracket beats until incomes rise above $90,000 (they give away 8.8 percent).

In fact, in absolute terms, the poorest Christians give away more dollars than all but the wealthiest Christians." (Christanity Today Dec 2008 Vol 52. No.12)

BECOMING A FRIEND OF GOD

According to scripture, Abraham was called the friend of God. (James 2:23) It should be our goal to also be considered a friend of God. Since God is not a respecter of persons, and never changes, it is possible for this occur. (Heb 13:8) We just need to qualify ourselves for such a distinct honor. Now, what does it take?

The First thing to know is the true character of God. You must do this on your own. Do not allow others to do this for you. You need to separate yourself, with God, to allow Him to disclose His true nature to you. God called Abraham to leave his country and family. (Gen 12:1) Moses fled into the desert of Arabia, and lived the life of a Sheppard. It was during this period, of isolation, he received the call of God through His angel. (Ex 2:11-25) The Apostle Paul, after his conversion, spent three years in Arabia, before formally beginning his ministry. (Gal 1:15-17) This is the process God utilizes for all those He uses to make an impact in this world.

MANY ARE CALLED FEW ARE CHOSEN

It is God's desire that all of His children be in an intimate relationship with Him. However, He realizes that most will not commit themselves. On several occasions, Jesus spoke on this topic. (Matt 16:20; 22: 14) In the Old Testament, God desired that the entire nation of Israel be a kingdom of priests to Him. (Ex 19: 5-6) However, once the people realized what it would cost them; they relegated the duties to Moses and the tribe of Levi. (Ex 20:18-21)

Another example is found in the New Testament in the book of Mark. A young man, who had much wealth, approached Jesus about the issue of eternal life. From his questions, he believed in Jesus. Jesus answered his questions, and the rich young man was happy because he felt he was qualified. However, when Jesus invited the young man to follow him, he became sad. The young man was instructed to give up his wealth. He did not want to let go of the one thing which was keeping him from a closer relationship with God.

It is my contention, that Jesus had special plans for this young man; because according to the scriptures, Jesus looked at him and loved him. (Mark 10:21) Maybe, Jesus planned for him to take Judas Iscariot spot? Who knows? What I do know, is that the young man decline the call. (Mark 10:22) Instead of trying to reason with the young man, Jesus watched him walk away.

There are several lessons to be learned from this. God will not violate your right to chose. You were created to be a free moral agent, which means you have the right to chose. God will respect that right, even if it is to your detriment. The second lesson is that if you chose to commit to God, he will reward you. (Mark 10:29-31) God promises rewards to those who believe in Him and act in the faith. (Heb 11:6)

COUNT THE COST

Finally, once you have separated yourself, and God starts to reveal His goodness to you, expect some persecution to come your way. The enemy will come against you, to discourage you and discredit God's revelations to you. He will use whatever he can to get you to doubt God and turn away. He realizes that you are now a threat to him and his kingdom. He does not want to see you get blessed, because he knows what will happen if others see the positive changes in your life. That is why Jesus admonished his disciples, in the story of the rich young ruler, that with all the blessings they would receive; because of their obedience; they would also receive persecution. (Mark 10:29-31)

God will use these trials to strengthen you in your faith. So, when you face your trials, look at them as exercises to build your faith. It's just like going to the fitness center to build your muscles. I find, when you look at the trial from this perspective, it is easier to go through. Also, keep in mind the promises of God and know that no matter how great the pressure or temptation, you win; because, you are more than a conqueror in Christ Jesus! (Rom 8:37)

THE STRATEGY OF THE ENEMY

Before closing this book, I want to give you some information to use; when the enemy of your faith comes knocking on your door. Just the fact that you have read this book or attended one of my workshops makes you a prime target. Up to this point, you have not been a real threat to him. But now, since your spiritual eyes have been opened, the enemy will do everything in his power to discourage you from putting what you have learned into practice.

This is his most common technique. He will use a crisis to dissuade you from continuing in your walk of faith. Why does he do this? Because, he does not want the seed of faith, to take root in your unconscious mind and produce a crop. (Mark 4:3-7) He will use a perceived offense, stronghold, or some type of crisis to keep the Word from producing a crop in your life.

When you read the entire account given in Mark the fourth chapter, you will see that only one out of the four seeds produced a crop of any kind. It will be the same with any teaching you receive in faith. Not everyone will get the harvest, because they allowed the enemy's strategies to succeed. However, if you are aware of his strategy, then he will not succeed. You will be able to recognize what he is doing and beat him down with the Word of God. (Eph 6:10-17)

As a believer you must never forget that you are in a spiritual battle, and your enemy is relentless. He will use every opportunity to get you to use your words against you and nullify the words of faith you have spoken. (Luke 4:13) He knows that his only weapon is his power to deceive you into using your power against yourself. If you are aware of this, then when the hardship comes, you will be equipped to overcome it (1 Peter 5:5-11)

We must understand that situations in life some time comes for no other reason than to test us. God will use situations to test us, even though He did not create the situation. Testing is part of the process God uses to expose to us what is really in our heart. What happened to Jesus, before he started his ministry? He was tested. According to the scriptures, Jesus was led by the Holy Spirit into the wilderness to be tempted. (Matt 4:1) The purpose of him going into the wilderness was to see if he could stand the test. What does a company do when it has a new product? They will run a test to see if the product will do what they advertise.

NEW COVENANT REALITIES

Recently, the Holy Spirit made me aware of the position that I have with God through Christ Jesus. I had known about my position in Christ Jesus through reading the Word of God and hearing numerous preaching on the subject. However, this time it was **rhema** in my spirit. In other words, something clicked on the inside of me, and I understood what it really meant. Sometimes, we can hear something and just accept it without really understanding the nuances.

This particular morning, I was given a deeper understanding of what it means to, "be in Christ Jesus". It was so simple, yet it was so hard for me to accept in the past. I think part of the reason why it was so difficult for me to comprehend was that I was placing limits on God's love for me. I was trying to understand God's love for me, from a human perspective, instead of from His perspective. Once I realized that God is love (1 John 4:8), and read the characteristics of love in (1 Cor 13:3-8), I understood that God's love for me was without limit.

I understood the great lengths God went through to redeem me. I understood what it meant to be "In Christ Jesus". According to Dr. Clarence Hale, the term "In Christ Jesus" appears 174 times in the New Testament; Dr. Hale, reports that the term, "In Christ" can be translated 241 different ways. However, I want to focus on just one of the ways, it can be translated. This to me is the most important translation, because it conveys the relational status we have with God Almighty.

In the book of Ephesians, The Apostle Paul speaks of the positional relationship we have with God through Christ Jesus. For example, Paul states that we have an inheritance, because we are "In Christ Jesus". (Eph 1:9-12) Then later Paul states, that we have been raised with Jesus and seated in the Heavenly Holy of Holies. (Eph 2:6) He also states that we are God's workmanship. (Eph 2:10)

Just take a moment to ponder on all the above mentioned statements made by the Apostle Paul, recorded in the Book of Ephesians. This is only a few of the descriptions, which convey, what we are in the eyes of God. Everyone, who has made Jesus their Lord and Savior; has the same relationship with God, whether they realize it or not.

However, there are some believers that have taken the time to find out what their "New Covenants" rights are; and have taken advantage of the benefits. Then, there are those believers, who are completely ignorant. Unfortunately, for them, they will struggle through life; like just any other non-believer, when they could have been sitting at the Father's table; experiencing "heaven on earth". (Due 11:12)

It is to our benefit, to find out exactly, what our "New Covenants" rights are; so that we can experience some of the blessings that God has provided for us. What the term, "In Christ" means, is when God looks at us, He sees His Son instead of us. Jesus told his disciples that if they would love him and keep his words, he and his father would come to abide in them. (John 14:23) Because of this, they could ask for anything in the name of Jesus, and it would be done for them. (John 14:13-14)

Again, The Apostle John, states that because we are "In Christ Jesus" we have confidence, to go boldly before the throne of God; and ask for anything that is in accordance of His will, and know that it will be given to us. (1 John 5:14-15)

WHY AREN'T YOUR PRAYERS BEING ANSWERED?

The main reason why many people's prayers do not get answered is because of sin. Sin robs us of fellowship with God. Just like Adam, in the Garden of Eden, we have the tendency to run away from God; and hide ourselves from Him. I think one of the reasons we do this, is because God cannot tolerate sin. The closer we come into His Presence, the more we realize how sinful we are. That is where the "blood of Christ" comes into play. The precious Blood of Jesus cleans and purges us in order that we can step boldly into His presence. (Rom 3:25, 5:9)

Once we establish this mindset in our consciousness, we can go into the Presence of the Father any time we like with confidence, just like Jesus. We can make request, just like Jesus did, and expect to receive what we have asked for. In order for this to occur, you must understand the cleansing power, of the Blood of Jesus. You must understand that once you have made Jesus the LORD of your life, God immediately forgets your past sins. (Ish 43:25) Because when He looks at you, God sees His Son; because, we are in Him.

Many preachers will not teach this for a myriad of reasons; one of them being ignorance, due to their religious indoctrination. However, the Holy Spirit will not allow for this.

According the scriptures, God promised, that in the New Covenant, He would put His Spirit in us; and write His laws in our heart. Furthermore, He would have an intimate relationship with us. This is the New Covenant reality. (Jer 31:31-34) This is available to us right now! Are you experiencing it? If not, why? Are you allowing sin to rob you of this relationship? Are you allowing the enemy, to keep you away from God? Or, are you just ignorant of your new covenant rights? Well, after reading this you cannot be ignorant any longer; so, what is your excuse?

COGNITIVE RESTRUCTURING STRATEGIES FOR A BREAKTHROUGH

In conclusion, I would like to summarize what we have learned. This information will be useful to review regularly, while on your journey to your promised land.

- You must understand the power of your words; and realize that your words are the vehicle used to create your world and change your circumstances. Your words create images that are used by the unconscious mind (spirit) to create your reality. **(Mark 11:23-24)**

- You must act on your profession of faith. Your action should be representative of what you have believed for. **(James 2: 22-25)**

- You must believe that God delights in you being prosperous. **(Psalms 35:27)**

- You must understand the importance of renewing your mind by studying and mediating on the promises and word of God daily. By doing this, you will place yourself in a position for God to prosper you. **(3 John 1:2)**

- Change your perspective on how your view hardships. Instead of seeing them as problems, view them as opportunities. It is only through hardships we grow. Hardships are the vehicle God sometimes uses to build our faith. **(James 1:2-3)**

- Know that you are part of God's plan. God wants your life to be a display of His goodness and glory. **(Eph 3:9-13)**

- Nothing is impossible with God. **(Luke 1:37)** Don't be afraid to dream, the impossible dream. Don't allow others to define your reality. Realize that God is looking for people who will believe His promises and His words in spite of their circumstances. **(Rom 4:20-21)**

- You must understand the importance of basing your faith on God and His promises. God is a spiritual being (John 4:24), and He is not moved by our circumstances but by faith. **(Heb 11:6)**

- Faith is a force, which is not detectable by the natural senses. It is a spiritual substance that is able to manifest itself in the physical realm. **(Heb 11:3)**

FINAL ADMONISHMENT

This concludes the book; I hope that you have received revelations that will assist you in claiming your Promise Land and becoming what God created you to be. There are a few things I would like to leave you with.

Do not be passive in your faith. You must not confuse faith with belief. Faith is a noun and belief is an action. Your belief activates your faith. In the scriptures it says that we must be aggressive in obtaining the Kingdom of God. (Matt 11:12) This means you must put action or effort into what you have released your faith to do.

You must spend time mediating on the Word of God, and His promises to you. This is how you will be able to strengthen your faith, during times of testing. This is how you will develop, the same type of faith, which Abraham had. (Rom 4:19-21)

Understand the power of your words. Your words are the reflection, of what is in your inner man. (Matt 12:34) Your words, determine your destiny. (Prov 18:21) You must watch what you profess and confess, because you can use your words, to our own detriment. (Matt 12: 35-37)

Trust the process. When God gives you a promise, it will not happen over night. Sometimes, you might have to wait years for the manifestation to occur. But there is a reason for it. You are not ready! Trust God, and realize that, He knows what is best for you. (Prov 1:32)

Know that nothing is impossible with God; and He is faithful to His Word. If God has made a promise to you, He will make sure it happens. (Heb 6:18)

MY JOURNEY

I was raised in a dysfunctional home where I witnessed the horrors of domestic, violence at a young age. I was sexually molested by my teenage baby sitter, before the age of ten. Because of the aforementioned, I was some what of a behavioral problem in school. I was labeled a "slow learner" and was placed in a special education classes. From all accounts I should have wound up in the penal system, like most children that come from this type of environment; but God had other plans for me.

God's hand was upon me in spite of myself. Even though it would be much later in my life, that I would accept Jesus; as my LORD and Savior, I felt His presence with me. God blessed me, with athletic ability to excel in sports. As result, I received an athletic scholarship to the University of Arizona to play football. After graduating with my Bachelor's of Arts in Psychology, I was fortunate enough to play in the NFL with the San Diego Chargers.

It wasn't until I was released by the Chargers, that I accepted Jesus as my LORD and Savior. From that moment on, I have learned of His great love for me. Like the prodigal son, I left the father's care, to chase after the things of this world but like the father of the prodigal son, God was waiting with open arms, for me to come to my senses.

I believe God has used my experiences, to equip me for what He wants me to do. That is to empower His people to live up to their God given potential.

Beloved, I wish above all things that thou mayest prosper and be in health, even as your souls prosper. (3 John 1:2)KJV

For more information about myself or to contact me please go to my website **www.olcoutreach.org.**

REFERENCES

Christianity Today, December 2008 Vol, 52 No. 12

Corey Gerald, Theory and Practice of Counseling and Psychotherapy, third edition Wiley Publishers 1986

DSM IV Desk Reference, Published by the American Psychiatric Assoc. Washington, DC Oct 2002

English Standard Version Bible, Published by Good News Publishers 2001

King James Version Bible, AMG Publishers, Chattanooga, TN 1991

Merriam-Webster's Dictionary, Merriam-Webster, Incorporated, Springfield Mass, 2006

www.crosswalk.com/marriage/11568721